MIMO.

W9-AUQ-119

Purchase S.East. '4.45 40

LEGENDARY HEROES
OF THE WILD WEST

BUFFALO BILL CODY
SHOWMAN OF THE WILD WEST

William R. Sanford & Carl R. Green

ENSLOW PUBLISHERS, INC.

44 Fadem Road
Box 699
Springfield, N.J. 07081
U.S.A.

P.O. Box 38
Aldershot
Hants GU12 6BP
U.K.

7178

Library of Congress Cataloging-in-Publication Data

Sanford, William R. (William Reynolds), 1927–
    Buffalo Bill Cody: showman of the Wild West / William
R. Sanford and Carl R. Green.
        p. cm — (Legendary heroes of the Wild West)
    Includes bibliographical references (p.) and index.
    ISBN 0-89490-646-1
    1. Buffalo Bill, 1846–1917—Juvenile literature. 2. Pioneers—
West (U.S.)—Biography—Juvenile literature. 3. Entertainers—
United States—Biography—Juvenile literature. 4. West (U.S.)—
Biography—Juvenile literature. 5. Buffalo Bill's Wild West Show—
History—Juvenile literature. I. Green, Carl R. II. Title.
III. Series: Sanford, William R. (William Reynolds), 1927–
Legendary heroes of the Wild West.
F594.B63S36   1996
978'.02'092—dc20   95-32147
                                                        CIP
                                                        AC

Printed in the United States of America

10 9 8 7 6 5 4 3 2 1

Illustration Credits: Buffalo Bill Historical Center, Cody, Wyoming, pp. 14,
15, 23, 24, 26, 28, 31, 35, 37, 41; Buffalo Bill Memorial Museum, Lookout
Mountain, Colorado, pp. 8, 10, 27, 33; Denver Public Library, Western
History Collection, pp. 6, 16, 40; William R. Sanford and Carl R. Green, pp.
18, 20.

Cover Illustration: Paul Daly

CONTENTS

Authors' Note 4

1 Riding for the Pony Express 5

2 A Boy Grows Up Fast
   on the Frontier 9

3 A Civil War Soldier Finds a Bride 13

4 A Buffalo Hunter Turns Celebrity 17

5 Hunting with a Grand Duke 21

6 On Stage and Off 25

7 Buffalo Bill's Wild West Show 30

8 Performing for the Queen 34

9 A Showman to the End 38

Notes by Chapter 42

Glossary 45

More Good Reading
   About Buffalo Bill 46

Index 47

Authors' Note

This book tells the true story of William F. Cody. Most people know him by his famous nickname, Buffalo Bill. Bill was one of the Wild West's greatest heroes. He was a brave and resourceful scout, a buffalo hunter, and a distinguished showman. During his lifetime, he was the subject of hundreds of dime novels. In more recent years, he has been brought to life in dozens of films and television productions. You may doubt that one man could pack so much adventure into a single lifetime. If so, rest easy. All of the events described in this book really happened.

1

RIDING FOR THE PONY EXPRESS

Fourteen-year-old Bill Cody crouched low as his horse galloped across Wyoming Territory. Like all Pony Express riders, he was paid to cover fifteen miles an hour. Horse Creek station lay a mile behind the young mail carrier. A fresh horse waited for him at Sweetwater Bridge.

Bill's horse thundered through a ravine. Without warning, a band of Native American warriors swarmed down the sides of the ravine. Rifles barked. Bullets whistled past Bill's head. The boy flattened himself on the horse's back. Reaching for more speed, he put spurs and whip to his mount. Luckily, he was riding one of the station's fastest horses.

His pursuers were two miles behind when Bill pulled up at Sweetwater Bridge. Instead of a fresh horse, he found a dead station keeper. The corral was empty. Bill

Fourteen-year-old Bill Cody proved his courage and endurance when he carried the mail for the Pony Express. On one ride, Bill saved his scalp by outriding a band of Native American warriors. On another day, he earned his boss's respect by making a bone-jarring round trip of 322 miles.

~~~~~~~~~~~~~

pushed his tired horse on to Plant's Station. A change of mounts was waiting for him. "I finished the trip without any further adventure," he wrote later.[1]

Bill rode for the firm of Russell, Majors, and Waddell. He was one of eighty riders who carried the mail from St. Joseph, Missouri, to California. The old mail route had curved southward through Texas and Arizona. Letters sent by that route took twenty-five days to reach San

Francisco. The Pony Express cut delivery time to ten days. The riders galloped across prairie, desert, and mountains.

Wagon master George Chrisman gave Bill his first job with the Pony Express. The boy assured his boss that he had been raised in the saddle. As a test, Chrisman assigned Bill to a short forty-five-mile leg out of Julesburg, Colorado. Bill proved his worth by finishing the rugged ride on time. His light weight, he said, was easy on the horses. Some months later, stage agent Alf Slade took a liking to the boy. Slade put Bill on the seventy-six-mile leg from Red Buttes to Three Crossings, Wyoming.

Like all the riders, Bill carried mail in pouches sewn into a sheet of leather. This *mochila* was cut to fit over the saddle's wooden frame. As Bill sped into a station, he pulled the *mochila* out from under him. After a quick dismount, he threw it onto a waiting horse. A station agent scribbled on his time card. A moment later Bill was off again.[2]

Bone-jarring rides of seventy-six miles were all in a day's work. Bill earned Slade's praise with a greater show of endurance. On reaching Three Crossings one day, he found that the relief rider had been killed in a brawl. Bill jumped on a fresh horse and set out for Rocky Ridge, eighty-five miles away. There he picked up the eastbound *mochila* and retraced his route. The round trip totaled 322 miles. "My boy," Slade told him, "you're a brick, and no mistake. That was a good run you made."[3] Coming from a tough boss like Slade, that was high praise.

In June 1861, Bill left the Pony Express to be with his

ailing mother. On October 24, workers finished the first cross-country telegraph line. Sending a message from New York to San Francisco now took only minutes. The Pony Express could not compete. The bankrupt line shut down in November.

Years later, Buffalo Bill brought the Pony Express back to life in his Wild West show. Daring riders helped cheering crowds relive the drama of the horseback mail service. Buffalo Bill knew the Pony Express as well as anyone alive. As the teenage Bill Cody, he had *been* a Pony Express rider.

Young Bill Cody spent only a few months as a Pony Express rider. Later, he went on to become a legendary western hero. Adoring fans all over the world called him by his nickname, Buffalo Bill. Here, Bill poses for the camera in the fringed buckskins of a frontier scout.

2

A BOY GROWS UP FAST
ON THE FRONTIER

Like many young people of their day, Isaac Cody and Mary Ann Laycock wanted elbow room. In 1840, the newlyweds moved to the Iowa Territory. The young couple built a four-room log cabin near Le Claire. Samuel was born in 1841, Julia in 1843. On February 26, 1846, Mary gave birth to William Frederick Cody. Her pet name for the baby was Billy. His brother and sisters called him Willy. As a teenager, the boy set the matter straight. He told people to call him Bill.[1]

Danger was a fact of life on a frontier farm. In 1853 a skittish mare reared up, threw Samuel, and fell back on him. The boy died the next day. To take his wife's mind off her grief, Bill's father moved the family to Kansas.

At Fort Leavenworth Bill saw his first Native Americans. He felt an even greater thrill when he saw soldiers drilling their well-trained horses. Before long his father

Mary Ann Cody dressed four-year-old Bill in his best outfit for this portrait. A few years later, his father moved the family to a frontier region of Kansas. There, Bill leaned to ride, shoot, and throw a lasso.

gave him a half-wild Indian pony named Prince. Horace Billings, Bill's uncle, helped the boy tame his new mount. Horace also taught Bill how to throw a lasso.

For a while, all went well. The Codys built a seven-room cabin at Salt Creek Valley. Isaac won a contract to supply hay to Fort Leavenworth.

In May 1854, Congress passed a law that opened years of strife. The law gave Kansas the right to choose to be a free state or a slave state. That set off a race to settle the territory. Proslavers and antislavers hurried to stake their claims.

That September, Bill and his father passed a proslavery rally. The leaders stopped Isaac and forced him to speak to the crowd. His father, Bill wrote later, said he opposed the spread of slavery. That was too much for one proslave hothead. The man stabbed Isaac in the chest. Eight-year-old Bill helped carry his father to the nearby trading post.[2]

Isaac survived, but bands of proslavers were hunting for him. He went into hiding. Unable to find their man, the raiders stole the Codys' livestock and burned their hay. Their anger did not stop there. Bill and his sisters had been going to a country school. The teacher fled when proslavers threatened to burn the school.

To help feed the family, Bill planted ten acres of corn. When he was not tending the crop, he hunted rabbits and squirrels. He needed his hunting rifle the night a killer came looking for his father. Isaac, Bill knew, was upstairs, too sick to leave his bed. The boy stood guard at the head of the stairs, ready to shoot. Bill's mother calmed the man by feeding him a good supper. He left at last, still vowing to kill "her damned abolitionist husband."[3]

Isaac died of pneumonia in the spring of 1857. The Codys blamed his death on the old stab wound. With Isaac gone, the family was short of cash. Mary sold the horses and put the farm up for rent. A neighbor hired Bill to haul supplies to Leavenworth for fifty cents a day. When that job ended, Bill found work carrying messages. The pay was good, but he hated the sitting and waiting. John Willis, a friendly wagon boss, gave him a better job. Bill tended Willis's oxen each time they returned from a trip.

That winter Mary sent Bill back to school. The fee was two dollars a month. In the spring, he fell hard for pretty Mary Hyatt. To please her, he built a playhouse in the schoolyard. An older boy named Steve Gobel kicked it down. In the fight that followed, Steve pinned Bill against a wall. Bill pulled out a pocketknife and slashed the bully's thigh. Steve ran to the teacher, screaming that he had been killed. That night a constable came looking for Bill.

Bill hid out while John Willis talked to Mary. She agreed that Bill should join Willis on a trip to Fort Kearny. "The trip was a most enjoyable one for me," Bill reported. "No incidents of note occurred on the way."[4] The fight was forgotten by the time the wagon train returned.

3
A CIVIL WAR SOLDIER FINDS A BRIDE

〜〜〜〜〜〜〜〜〜〜

The conflict over slavery soon engulfed the nation. The first shots of the Civil War rang out in April 1861. Bill Cody, fresh from his work for the Pony Express, could have served as a drummer boy. Many fifteen-year-olds wore Northern blue or Southern gray. It was his mother, ill with consumption, who stood in his way. She made him promise not to join up while she lived.[1]

The promise kept Bill out of uniform but not out of trouble. Kansas had become a free state, but slavery still existed across the border in Missouri. When a band of Kansans planned a raid on Missouri farms, Bill rode with them. Perhaps he hoped to avenge his father's death. The raiders, it turned out, were mostly out to steal horses.

As Bill wrote later, "We didn't let our consciences trouble us very much."[2] Mary Cody learned that several raiders had been sent to jail. She ordered Bill to quit the band. He obeyed.

Heading west again, Bill met two of the Wild West's greatest heroes. The first was a scout named Wild Bill Hickok. Hickok hired the boy to help haul freight. In St. Louis, the two lost all their money betting on a horse race. In the spring of 1862, Bill served as guide and scout with the Ninth Kansas Volunteers. The troop's task was to keep the Santa Fe trail open. In New Mexico, he was awed by the famous mountain man Kit Carson. Years later, Bill named his son Kit Carson Cody.

In 1863 Bill left the volunteers to join a wagon train bound for Denver. Word reached him there that his mother was gravely ill. He returned in time to say goodbye before she died.

The Seventh Kansas Volunteers came home on leave

in February 1864. His friends in the troop urged Bill to join up. He turned them down, but joined them for a drinking spree. "One morning I awoke to find myself a soldier," he

Still in his teens, Buffalo Bill became friends with one of the Wild West's greatest heroes. Wild Bill Hickok (shown here, dressed in his city best) hired Bill to work with him hauling freight. During the Civil War, the two met again while both were scouting behind enemy lines.

Bill Cody cut a dashing figure in his role of frontier scout. There was more to the man than good looks, however. He was a superb horseman and a crack shot. Cavalry troopers fighting for their lives were happy to have Bill and his Winchester rifle close by.

wrote. "I did not remember how or when I had enlisted, but I saw I was in for it."[3]

Army records say that Private Cody served in Company H. His hair and eyes are listed as brown, his height as five feet ten inches. In June the regiment marched south to guard a key rail line. On July 14, Bill took part in a major battle. The Union army stopped the Confederates that day at Tupelo, Mississippi.

In September the regiment moved north. Private Cody was detailed to serve as a scout. On one trip behind rebel lines, he described a meeting with a gray-clad stranger. To his surprise, the "Southerner" turned out to be Wild Bill Hickok. Hickok gave him a packet of reports to take back. Did those reports help the North turn back a Southern thrust toward St. Louis? Bill thought they did.[4]

That winter the army assigned Bill to a St. Louis hospital. In his off-duty hours, he met Louisa Federici. Bill wrote, "I adored her above any young lady I had ever seen."[5] As a joke on one of her boyfriends, the two pretended to be engaged.

Bill left the service in September, still a private. Short of cash, he took a job driving horses to Fort Kearny, Nebraska. Next he worked as a stagecoach driver. It was Louisa's letters that drew him east again. The joke engagement had turned serious. She was urging him to give up his wild life. Keep your promise to marry me, she said.[6]

Bill was dressed in western buckskins when he reached St. Louis. He was growing a mustache and a goatee. On March 6, 1866, he married Louisa. That same day the newlyweds boarded a steamboat for Leavenworth. They were in love, but they were not well matched. Louisa wanted a quiet life. Only twenty years old, Bill yearned for open spaces and adventure.

In an attempt to please Louisa, Bill opened a hotel. The venture lasted only six money-losing months. Bill sold out and headed back to the plains. A tearful Louisa returned to St. Louis.

~~~~~~~~~~~~~~~~~~

Bill Cody married Louisa Federici soon after the end of the Civil War. Marriage soon revealed what the wartime romance had concealed: the two were very different. Louisa wanted a quiet, settled home life. Bill tried to give her that kind of life, but soon gave up. He could not resist the call of the frontier.

4

A BUFFALO HUNTER TURNS CELEBRITY

The turning point in Bill's life came in 1867. Clear at last of Louisa's pleas to settle down, he went to work for the railroad. One day he was grading a railbed. His horse, Brigham, was pulling the heavy grader. When Bill spotted a herd of buffalo, he unhitched the horse. Rifle in hand, he set out to shoot some buffalo for the work crew's supper.

As he neared the herd, Bill met some army officers. They laughed and told him that his workhorse would never catch the herd. One of the men offered to shoot a buffalo for him. That was when Bill dropped Brigham's reins, leaving both hands free. Moments later he was closing on the herd. The soldiers fell back, unable to match Brigham's speed. Bill dropped the closest buffalo with a single shot. One by one, he killed ten more. The hunt ended, he gave the officers a share of the meat.[1]

That fall, the railroad hired Bill to shoot twelve buffalo a day. The meat was used to feed the work crews. Bill enjoyed the work. At $1.67 a head, he earned $500 a month. Later, he wrote, "During my engagement as hunter for the company—a period of less than eighteen months—I killed 4,280 buffaloes."[2] The work crews made up a song to sing when he passed:

Buffalo Bill, Buffalo Bill
Never missed and never will.
Always aims and shoots to kill
And the company pays his buffalo bill.[3]

Bill said it was these workmen who first called him Buffalo Bill. Others suggest it was the army officers at Fort

Buffalo Bill earned his nickname as a buffalo hunter. The railroad, which fed its work crews with buffalo meat, paid Bill $1.67 for each of his kills. In this old engraving, the hunter is using Bill's technique of riding into the herd and firing from close range.

Hayes. A third story credits dime novel author Ned Buntline. As the story goes, Buntline needed a new hero for his novels. At Fort Sedgwick he heard about Bill Cody's exploits. When Buntline found him, Bill was asleep under a wagon. Their meeting led to an 1869 tale called *Buffalo Bill, King of Border Men*.[4] The novel was the first of many. Over the years, Buffalo Bill was featured in over five hundred dime novels.

Bill claimed that he won $300 and the title of Champion Buffalo Hunter in a shootoff. Officers at Fort Wallace backed their scout, Billy Comstock. The men at Fort Hayes put their money on Bill. During the eight-hour match, the hunters closed on four small herds. Thanks to Brigham, Bill was able to drive his buffalo in a tight circle. Comstock chased his buffalo straight across the plain. Bill got off more shots—and he seldom missed. The final score read Buffalo Bill 69, Comstock 46.[5]

In May 1868, Bill signed on as an army scout. The job soon tested him to the utmost. In one sixty-hour ride, he carried dispatches across three hundred fifty miles of Native American territory. General Philip Sheridan was impressed. He named Bill as chief scout for the Fifth Cavalry. The pay was equal to that paid an army colonel. Bill said that if he was drawing the pay, he deserved the title. In later life, he often called himself Colonel Cody.[6]

Bill lived the rugged life of a scout for the next four years. In 1872 he was called on to help fight the Sioux. While scouting with six soldiers, Bill found the camp of a Sioux war party. Both sides opened fire. Deadeye shooting killed three warriors. As the soldiers charged, the other warriors tried to flee. The pursuit almost ended when the soldiers' horses balked at jumping a creek. Bill's horse cleared it and took up the chase. Moments later he shot two of the Sioux from their mounts. The others fled. For his bravery, Bill won the Congressional Medal of Honor.

History writes a strange footnote to that story. In 1916 Congress voted to strike Bill's name from the list of medal holders. What was the reason? The nation's highest honor was meant only for members of the armed forces. Bill, hired as a scout, had been a civilian. Congress reversed itself and restored the medal in 1989—seventy-two years after Bill's death.[7]

In 1872 Bill was very much alive. That fall, friends put him on the ballot for the Nebraska legislature. To his surprise, he won by forty-four votes. His career in politics did not last long. A recount gave the seat to his opponent.[8] Bill was free to return to the life he loved best.

In 1869 Ned Buntline featured Buffalo Bill in a western story. The public loved it. Other writers raced to invent ever wilder adventures for the new hero. In 1881, any young reader with the price of "half a dime" could enjoy this fanciful story about Bill's early years.

5
HUNTING WITH A GRAND DUKE

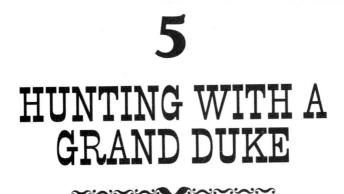

During his years as a scout, the army found other uses for Bill's talents. The Fifth Cavalry was sent to Arizona to fight the Apache late in 1871. Bill did not join the troop. That summer, he had served as guide for a party of wealthy easterners. The hunt had been a smashing success. In November General Sheridan sent Bill to take part in a once-in-a-lifetime event.

The Grand Duke Alexis, son of the Russian czar, was touring the United States. When the duke said he wanted to shoot buffalo, the government ordered a royal hunt. At Sheridan's command, Bill took charge. First he picked out a campsite near Fort McPherson, Nebraska. Soldiers hurried to build Camp Alexis on a grassy knoll above Red Willow Creek. As Bill would say, it was a "dude's camp." The tents had wooden floors, carpets, and wood-burning stoves.

To add zest, Bill asked Spotted Tail, a Sioux chief, to join the hunt. The chief brought a large band of warriors with him. On the first night in camp, the Sioux staged a war dance. The grand duke and his party were delighted. The grand duke even flirted with a Sioux maiden.[1]

January 14, 1872, was the grand duke's twenty-first birthday. He rode out mounted on Bill's best horse, Buckskin Joe. Shortly after nine o'clock, the party sighted a small herd of buffalo. The grand duke rode to within twenty feet and fired six wild pistol shots. None hit their mark. Bill handed the grand duke his pistol. Six more shots produced six more misses.

By custom, the royal guest had to make the first kill. Bill gave the grand duke his rifle and slapped Buckskin Joe on the rump. The well-trained horse sprinted forward. As he closed on a big bull, the grand duke aimed and fired. The bull dropped. Grand Duke Alexis waved his hat as the rest of the party cheered.

A few news stories claimed that Bill killed the buffalo. Bill denied the story, as did others who were there. What is certain is that the grand duke toasted his kill with champagne. Bill later wrote, "I was in hopes that he would kill five or six more buffaloes . . . if a basket of champagne was to be opened every time he dropped one."[2]

Chinese lanterns hung from the trees above the camp that night. The camp chefs prepared a special meal. The first course was buffalo tail soup. Next came broiled fish, prairie dog sausage, and stewed rabbit. The grand duke ate a large tender slice of buffalo hump. The menu also

In 1872 Buffalo Bill organized a hunt for a royal visitor, the Grand Duke Alexis of Russia. In this painting, the grand duke (center, with pistol) had failed in his first attempt to bring down a buffalo. Minutes later, Bill (on white horse) handed Alexis his rifle. Thanks to the added firepower, the duke was able to kill one of the massive animals.

included roast elk, deer, and wild turkey. Champagne, whiskey, brandy, and ale flowed freely.[3]

The hunt lasted five days. In all, the grand duke bagged eight buffalo. A high point came the day the Sioux showed how they killed buffalo with bows and arrows. The grand duke rewarded Spotted Tail with a gift of one thousand barrels of tobacco. Each night the hunters gathered around blazing campfires. Bill kept the Russians spellbound with his stories.

On the last day, Bill rode to the train with the grand duke and General Sheridan. Four half-trained cavalry horses pulled the open carriage. Hearing that Bill had once been a stage driver, the grand duke asked him to take the reins. "Shake 'em up a little," Sheridan ordered. Bill soon had the team flying over the rough ground. Their speed increased when they hit a long downhill slope. Without a brake, Bill could only keep the horses running straight ahead. He claimed later that he covered three miles in six minutes. A shaken grand duke said he preferred to "go a little slower."[4]

On parting, the grand duke tried to give Bill a roll of greenbacks. Bill turned down the offer, but he did accept the grand duke's fine fur coat. Later, Alexis sent him a set of cuff links and a scarf pin. The pin, made in the shape of a buffalo head, was set with diamonds.

The world's press reported each day of the hunt. Buffalo Bill was becoming a household name. Bill Cody sensed that a door had opened for him.[5] The challenge was to use his fame to fatten his empty purse.

After Bill's success with the grand duke, wealthy eastern hunters lined up to hire him as a guide. This photo was taken at a camp on the Shoshone River in November 1901. Bill titled the print, "The life I love."

6

ON STAGE AND OFF

Bill made his first visit to New York in the spring of 1872. Ned Buntline took him to see a play based on his exploits. *Buffalo Bill, King of the Border Men* was one long tall tale. Bill drew the loudest cheers when he walked on stage to take a bow.

Buntline argued that Bill should become an actor. He promised to write a play tailored to his talents. Bill left to rejoin the Fifth Cavalry without giving him an answer.

As Buntline could see, Bill Cody was a performer. In his role as Buffalo Bill, he stood for the ideal Western man. He could ride and shoot, scout and hunt. His word was his bond. If he had a dollar, he would share it. He liked whiskey but never seemed to get drunk.

Working as a scout and guide kept Bill away from home for months at a time. His wife Louisa still yearned for a more peaceful existence. Also, she was jealous of the

7178

Adoring crowds filled the theaters when Buffalo Bill turned to acting. In 1872 Bill posed with his costars in Ned Buntline's western drama, Scouts of the Prairie. *From left to right: Buntline, Buffalo Bill, Giuseppina Morlacchi, and Texas Jack Omohundro.*

women who threw themselves at him. Yet it was Louisa who sewed his colorful costumes. She also raised their three children. When Bill was home, he spoiled Arta, Kit, and Orra Maude.

Bill met Buntline in Chicago that winter. *Scouts of the Prairie* opened a few days later to a packed house. When the curtain went up on December 16, Bill forgot his lines. Buntline saved the day by asking, "Where have you been,

Bill?" Bill told a few stories and warmed to the task. Before long the stage was filled with gunsmoke. Actors dressed as Native Americans died by the dozen. The critics thought the play was dreadful. The audience loved it.[1]

The play ran until June 1873. In September Bill opened a new play, *Scouts of the Plains*. Wild Bill Hickok, now a famous lawman, took Buntline's place. When bored, Wild Bill fired blanks at the legs of his fellow actors. The powder burns set them to hopping wildly.[2] Wild Bill left the stage after that single season.

Bill bought a home in Rochester, New York. He spent the summer of 1875 there with his family. Tragedy struck the following April while Bill was on tour. He rushed home when five-year-old Kit fell ill with scarlet fever. The boy died in his arms a few hours later.

In June 1876, trouble was brewing in the Dakota Territory. On June 17, the Sioux defeated General George Crook. Eight days

Kit Carson Cody, looking very much his father's son, was five when he posed for this photo. The boy fell ill with scarlet fever just a few weeks later. Bill rushed home to be with Kit, only to have the boy die in his arms.

later General George Custer fought Sitting Bull at the Little Big Horn. Custer's troops died to the last man. Bill was called west to scout for the Fifth Cavalry.

A thousand Cheyenne were riding to join Sitting Bull. The Fifth moved to head them off near War Bonnet Creek. On July 17, Bill led a small force in a flanking attack. He and a subchief named Yellow Hair opened fire at the same moment. Bill's shot smashed the Cheyenne's leg and killed his pony. Yellow Hair's slug missed. Bill's horse stumbled, but he rolled clear. Yellow Hair aimed, fired—and missed again. Bill's return shot found its mark.

Bill saw that Yellow Hair had tied a blonde scalp to his war bonnet. In his fury, Bill scalped the fallen subchief.

The troops of the Fifth Cavalry cheer as Bill cries, "First scalp for Custer!" Moments earlier, Bill and a Cheyenne subchief named Yellow Hair had exchanged shots at close range. In this painting, artist Robert Lindneaux shows Bill holding up Yellow Hair's war bonnet as a token of his victory.

Holding the war bonnet over his head, he cried, "The first scalp for Custer!"[3] That brief firefight ended the campaign. The outgunned Cheyenne returned to their homes.

Bill appeared in a new play that fall. He called it *The Red Right Hand, or Bill's First Scalp for Custer*. On stage, the shootout with Yellow Hair turned into a hand-to-hand duel. The next year's play was *Boy Chief of the Plains*. The public did not care that each play was much like the one before. Bill made enough money to buy a ranch near North Platte, Nebraska.

Bill knew his plays were rather silly. He dreamed of showing people the true West. His chance came in 1882. North Platte put him in charge of the Fourth of July show. Bill's Old Glory Blow-Out featured bronc riding, a stagecoach holdup, and a buffalo hunt. The applause convinced him that this was his type of show.

7
BUFFALO BILL'S WILD WEST SHOW

Bill put all his talent and cash into building a Wild West show. He and his partner, Dr. W. F. Carver, planned to "take the prairies and the Injuns and everything else right to 'em."[1] They hired cowboys, Native Americans, and sharp-shooters. Their agents rounded up a buffalo herd and bought bucking broncos. The livestock and equipment filled six boxcars.

The show opened in Omaha in May 1883. Posters bragged, "The Green Sward Our Carpet, Azure Canopy Our Canvas, No Tinsel, No Gilding, No Humbug!"[2] On show day, a cowboy band led a parade through the streets. The public, avid readers of dime novels, raced to buy tickets. Buffalo Bill was bringing them the real West!

The opening did not go smoothly. Some of the riders had spent too much time in the town's saloons. Even so, the crowd loved the show's wild energy. The cowboys showed off their riding and roping skills. The Native Americans raced bareback. The stagecoach robbery brought down the house. Bill thrilled his fans with a new act. Firing while riding at a gallop, he shattered glass balls thrown high by a second rider. In his first appearance, he hit eighty-seven out of one hundred balls.

A stressed-out Carver left after the first season. Showman Nate Salsbury moved in as Bill's new partner. With Salsbury taking care of the business end, Bill was free to improve the show. He bought new equipment and hired

BUFFALO BILL SHOOTING ON HORSEBACK AT FULL SPEED.

Buffalo Bill captured the excitement of western life in his Wild West shows. Here, a poster features Bill's show-stopping marksmanship. As the lead rider throws glass balls into the air, Bill spurs his horse to a gallop and shatters the balls with a volley of rifle fire.

new acts. One key addition was Johnny Baker. Back in Omaha, the nine-year-old had attached himself to Bill. Bill, in turn, treated Johnny like a son. Later, billed as the Cowboy Kid, Johnny put on a sharpshooting act.

Wild West fans could always count on five spectacles. Each year painted Native Americans performed war dances. Settlers defended their log cabin. Buffalo Bill saved the Deadwood stage. Pony Express riders carried the mail. A grand buffalo hunt always brought the crowd to its feet. Special effects included prairie fires, stampedes, and a cyclone.

Bill dressed to fit the popular image of a western scout. He wore his wide-brimmed white hat at a jaunty angle. A scarlet shirt set off his fringed white buckskin jacket. A matching sash circled his waist. Thigh-high black boots gleamed over white trousers. At his side he carried his trusty rifle. He took equal care in making the show look real. Author Mark Twain was convinced. Twain wrote, "Down to its smallest details the Show is genuine."[3]

In 1885, Buffalo Bill's Wild West Show added two stars. The first was sharpshooter Annie Oakley. Born in Ohio in 1860, Annie began shooting at age eight. At fifteen she outshot marksman Frank Butler. Butler soon became her husband and manager. Bill told his cast, "This little Missie here . . . she's the only white woman with our show. I want you boys to welcome and protect her."[4]

Annie was an artist with a rifle. At thirty paces, she could slice a playing card held edgewise. Women covered their eyes when Frank held up a dime between two fingers.

The public knew her as Annie Oakley, the finest sharpshooter of her age. Buffalo Bill called her Little Missy. Shown a playing card held edgewise, Annie could slice it in two from thirty paces. She was a featured act with Bill's Wild West show for many years.

Annie never missed. She even went Bill one better. She smashed flying glass balls, too—while sighting over her shoulder with a mirror.

Sitting Bull, the victor of Little Big Horn, also appeared that season. At first the aging chief had refused to join the show. Then Bill's agent spotted a photo of Annie in the chief's teepee. Sitting Bull, who called Annie "Little Sure Shot," had seen her perform. Told he would see her every day, Sitting Bull signed on for $50 a week. He also made good money selling autographed photos. When crowds booed him for his part in Custer's defeat, he ignored them. At season's end, Bill gave Sitting Bull a gray trick horse and a white sombrero.

In 1884 the show had nearly collapsed after a riverboat sank. Much of the equipment ended up on the bottom of the Mississippi. Rebuilding was slow work. The 1885 season, however, turned a $100,000 profit. As he neared forty, Bill looked for new worlds to conquer.

8

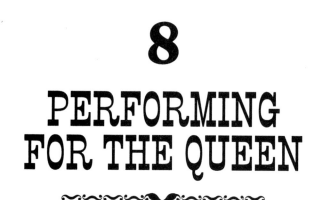

PERFORMING
FOR THE QUEEN

In 1887 the people of Europe were reading and talking about the Wild West. Sure of a warm welcome, Bill took his show to Great Britain. If the British wanted western romance, he would give it to them.

Travel to Europe meant a seventeen-day ocean voyage. The animals may have had the best of the trip. Most of the two-legged performers were seasick. Certain they were dying, the Native Americans chanted their death songs. Annie proved to be one of the better sailors. For several days, she had the ship's dining room almost to herself.

When the ship docked, the British waived some of their laws. The show's horses, buffalo, wild steers, elk, and mules were quarantined only briefly. The cast members were allowed to keep their firearms. Officials did draw the line at live bullets. Ammunition was stored at an army post and issued as needed.[1]

The show set up camp at Earl's Court on the west side of London. Rehearsals began in a twenty thousand seat arena. April rains chilled cast and crew. At night they huddled around coal fires in large, wooden-floored tents. To build interest, Bill gave away free tickets. The passes, which were pre-punched, were known as "Annie Oakleys." They looked as though Annie had used them as targets.

Edward, Prince of Wales, previewed the show. The future king was entranced. His praise led his mother, Queen Victoria, to ask Bill to perform at Windsor Castle. Bill had to turn her down. The show was too big to move for one performance. Victoria then surprised everyone. She announced that she would come to Earl's Court. This would be her first theater outing in twenty-six years. She had been in seclusion since the death of her husband.

The Queen's coach rolled into Earl's Court on May 11. Victoria, a stout woman of sixty-seven years old, took her seat in a box

Buffalo Bill's Wild West show was a great success in the United States. When he took the show abroad, he attracted even more attention. As this poster shows, Europe's royalty was captivated by Bill's version of life in the Wild West. Queen Victoria (top row, center) astonished everyone when she broke her long seclusion to attend the show.

Distinguished Visitors to Buffalo Bill's Wild West. London.1887.

trimmed with flags. Bill opened the show by carrying the Stars and Stripes into the arena. The Queen stood and bowed. With that bow, she became the first British ruler to salute the American flag.[2] Victoria had planned to stay only an hour. Caught up in the drama, she stayed for the entire seventy-five minutes. Afterward, she chatted with Bill, Annie, and Chief Red Shirt.

In June, Victoria asked to see the show again. Bill took his best acts to Windsor Castle for the command performance. The highlight came when he picked up the reins of the Deadwood stagecoach. Riding inside were the kings of Denmark, Greece, Belgium, and Saxony. The Prince of Wales sat beside him on the driver's seat. As the stagecoach jolted forward, a band of Native Americans swooped past. Riding bareback, they yelled and fired blanks. The ride gave birth to a popular joke. The stage, Bill liked to say, had carried Four Kings and the Royal Joker.[3]

The cowboys made their rodeo tricks look easy. England's top riders said they could stick on the broncs, too. The best lasted only thirty seconds before being bucked off. Two of the cowboys entered a six-day race against two English cyclists. For eight hours each day, the four riders circled a track at Islington. The cowboys used thirty horses, changing mounts each hour. When the race ended, the cowboys were two laps ahead.[4]

The show moved north in the fall. At Salford, Cody and Salsbury opened "the largest theater ever seen." The ten thousand-seat indoor arena was heated by steam and lighted by electricity. The cast performed in front of a huge painted backdrop of the western plains. The local paper reported, "Buffalo Bill has come, we have seen, and he has conquered."[5]

The homesick cast sailed for the United States in May 1888. The voyage was marred only by the death of Bill's horse, Old Charlie. The show reopened a few weeks later on Staten Island, New York. Not to be outdone by a British queen, President Grover Cleveland attended the opening.

Children were drawn to Buffalo Bill in every country he visited. Here, the aging hero shares a quiet moment with a circle of young fans. Unlike the tales told by many western storytellers, Buffalo Bill's stories were based on his own true adventures.

9

A SHOWMAN
TO THE END

In the fall of 1888, Bill rested at his ranch near North Platte. His life with Louisa had reached a low point. Their disputes centered on the fact that Bill would not, could not, settle down. Louisa, in turn, disliked travel. In time they no longer spoke.

In 1889 a Wild West fever swept Europe. Bill took his show to France, Spain, and Italy. Pope Leo XIII blessed the members of the cast. After a sellout year in Germany, the show played Holland and Belgium. Rumors spread that the Native Americans were badly treated. The rumors were false. Like the rest of the cast, they simply wanted to go home.[1]

Bill took the show home, but he was not finished with Europe. By May 1892 he was back in London, staging a third performance for Queen Victoria. Russian Cossacks and Argentine gauchos now rode beside American cowboys. Bill called the new show the Congress of the Rough Riders of the World.

The great showman had interests beyond the show. One was a new ranch in the Big Horn basin of Wyoming. In 1895 he helped lay out the nearby town that would bear his name. Six years later, the first train chugged into Cody. Bill joined in the celebration. When war broke out with Spain in 1898, fifty-two-year-old Bill Cody tried to join up. The fighting ended before the army took him up on his offer.

In 1903 Bill bought into a mine near Oracle, Arizona. Engineers promised a rich strike of gold, tungsten, and lead. For seven months, miners drilled around the clock. At last they hit a vein of ore. It proved to be low grade. By 1912, $500,000 of Bill's cash had vanished down the Campo Bonito mine.

At age sixty-six, Buffalo Bill was wearing out. His health was poor. His debts were mounting. He talked of retiring, but he could not afford to quit. An old friend, Major Gordon Lillie, talked him into making a three-year "farewell tour." The first year went well, then gate receipts fell. The public was learning to prefer movie versions of the Wild West.

Early in 1913, Bill borrowed $20,000. When he could not repay the loan, he had to auction off his animals and wagons. Next he tried his hand at making a movie. For one big scene, he hired Native Americans to restage the Battle of Wounded Knee. Just before the cameras rolled, Bill heard a chilling rumor. The young warriors wanted to

In old age, deeply in debt, Buffalo Bill traveled with a circus as a paid performer. Although he was in pain, he always managed to hold himself erect for his slow ride around the arena. When his final tour ended in November 1916, he had less than three months to live.

⁓⌇⁓⌇⁓⌇⁓⌇◆⁓⌇⁓⌇⁓⌇⁓

avenge the 1890 massacre. Instead of blanks, they were planning to use real bullets. Bill talked to the older chiefs, who kept the hot-heads under control.[2] In February 1914, Bill showed "The Indian Wars" to members of Congress. Then he took the film on the road for a brief tour.

To pay off old debts, Bill traveled with the Sells-Floto Circus. On his bad days he had to be helped onto his horse. Once he was in the saddle, he straightened his back. Only then did he ride into the spotlight. He made his final appearance in November 1916.

Bill spent his last days in Denver, too ill to travel. Death came on January 10, 1917. His friends knew he wanted to be buried on Cedar Mountain above Cody. Louisa claimed he had changed his mind. She buried him on Denver's Lookout Mountain.[3] The people of Cody built their own memorial. Their twelve-foot bronze statue shows Bill astride his black horse, Smokey.

Like all great heroes, Bill is still with us. He speaks across the years of courage, loyalty, and independence. Mounted on Buckskin Joe, he charges toward us. He holds a rifle in one hand, the reins in the other. His long hair streams behind him. It is an image that will last as long as memories of the Wild West endure.

Buffalo Bill wanted to be buried on Cedar Mountain, above the town of Cody, Wyoming. Louisa Cody ignored his request. She buried him on Denver's Lookout Mountain. The people of Cody responded by building their own memorial. G.T. Whitney's bronze statue, "The Scout," stands guard over the site.

NOTES BY CHAPTER

Chapter 1

1. William F. Cody, *The Life of Hon.William F. Cody, Known as Buffalo Bill* (New York: Indian Head Books, 1991; original edition 1879), pp. 105–106.

2. Don Russell, *The Lives and Legends of Buffalo Bill* (Norman, Okla.: University of Oklahoma Press, 1960), p. 46.

3. Cody, p. 105.

Chapter 2

1. Elizabeth Jane Leonard and Julia Cody Goodman, *Buffalo Bill, King of the Old West* (New York: Library Publishers, 1955), p. 73.

2. John Burke, *Buffalo Bill: The Noblest Whiteskin* (New York: Putnam, 1973), pp. 26–27.

3. Don Russell, *The Lives and Legends of Buffalo Bill* (Norman, Okla.: University of Oklahoma Press, 1960), p. 21.

4. William F. Cody, *The Life of Hon.William F. Cody, Known as Buffalo Bill* (New York: Indian Head Books, 1991; original edition 1879), p. 57.

Chapter 3

1. Don Russell, *The Lives and Legends of Buffalo Bill* (Norman, Okla.: University of Oklahoma Press, 1960), p. 56.

2. William F. Cody, *The Life of Hon.William F. Cody, Known as Buffalo Bill* (New York: Indian Head Books, 1991; original edition 1879), p. 127.

3. Cody, p. 135.

4. Cody, p. 137.

5. Russell, p. 73.

6. Henry Blackman Sell and Victor Weybright, *Buffalo Bill and the Wild West* (New York: Oxford University Press, 1955), p. 43.

Chapter 4

1. Keith Wheeler, *The Scouts* (Alexandria, Va.: Time-Life Books, 1978), pp. 202–203.

2. William F. Cody, *The Life of Hon.William F. Cody, Known as Buffalo Bill* (New York: Indian Head Books, 1991; original edition 1879), p. 162.

3. Elizabeth Jane Leonard and Julia Cody Goodman, *Buffalo Bill, King of the Old West* (New York: Library Publishers, 1955), p. 152.

4. Nellie Snyder Yost, *Buffalo Bill: His Family, Friends, Fame, Failures, and Fortunes* (Chicago: Sage Books, 1979), pp. 24–25.

5. Henry Blackman Sell and Victor Weybright, *Buffalo Bill and the Wild West* (New York: Oxford University Press, 1955), pp. 60–61.

6. John Burke, *Buffalo Bill: The Noblest Whiteskin* (New York: Putnam, 1973), p. 55.

7. Nancy Robison, *Buffalo Bill* (New York: Watts, 1991), p. 40.

8. Yost, pp. 66–67.

Chapter 5

1. Don Russell, *The Lives and Legends of Buffalo Bill* (Norman, Okla.: University of Oklahoma Press, 1960), p. 177.

2. William F. Cody, *The Life of Hon.William F. Cody, Known as Buffalo Bill* (New York: Indian Head Books, 1991; original edition 1879), p. 302.

3. Nellie Snyder Yost, *Buffalo Bill: His Family, Friends, Fame, Failures, and Fortunes* (Chicago: Sage Books, 1979), p. 54.

4. Cody, pp. 304–305.

5. John Burke, *Buffalo Bill: The Noblest Whiteskin* (New York: Putnam, 1973), p. 78.

Chapter 6

1. Henry Blackman Sell and Victor Weybright, *Buffalo Bill and the Wild West* (New York: Oxford University Press, 1955), p. 101.

2. Sell and Weybright, pp. 106–107.

3. William F. Cody, *The Life of Hon.William F. Cody, Known as Buffalo Bill* (New York: Indian Head Books, 1991; original edition 1879), p. 344.

Chapter 7

1. Henry Blackman Sell and Victor Weybright, *Buffalo Bill and the Wild West* (New York: Oxford University Press, 1955), p. 130.

2. Ibid., p. 135.

3. John Burke, *Buffalo Bill: The Noblest Whiteskin* (New York: Putnam, 1973), p. 164.

4. Don Russell, *The Lives and Legends of Buffalo Bill* (Norman, Okla.: University of Oklahoma Press, 1960), p. 313.

Chapter 8

1. Don Russell, *The Lives and Legends of Buffalo Bill* (Norman, Okla,: University of Oklahoma Press, 1960), p. 327.

2. John Burke, *Buffalo Bill: The Noblest Whiteskin* (New York: Putnam, 1973), pp. 175–176.

3. Nellie Snyder Yost, *Buffalo Bill: His Family, Friends, Fame, Failures, and Fortunes* (Chicago: Sage Books, 1979), p. 198.

4. Ibid., pp. 195–204.
5. Ibid., p. 206.

Chapter 9

1. Don Russell, *The Lives and Legends of Buffalo Bill* (Norman, Okla.: Unversity of Oklahoma Press, 1960), p. 341.
2. Henry Blackman Sell and Victor Weybright, *Buffalo Bill and the Wild West* (New York: Oxford Press, 1955), pp. 250–251.
3. John Burke, *Buffalo Bill: The Noblest Whiteskin* (New York: Putnam, 1973), pp. 290–291.

GLOSSARY

abolitionist—Someone who opposed the practice of slavery.

bankrupt—Financially ruined. A business goes bankrupt when it has more debts than assets.

broncos—Horses that have not been broken for riding. When a rider tries to mount a bronco, the horse does its best to buck the rider off.

buckskin—The skin of a male deer. Western scouts favored clothing made of buckskin.

cavalry—In Buffalo Bill's day, army units mounted on horseback. Today's cavalry soldiers ride in tanks and armored cars.

Civil War—The war between the North and the South, 1861–1865.

command performance—A show staged at the request of a king, queen, or other high-ranking figure.

constable—A law officer charged with keeping the peace in a town or village.

consumption—A common name for tuberculosis in the 1800s.

corral—A fenced area used to keep horses and cattle from straying.

czar—The emperor of Russia.

dime novels—Low-cost magazines that printed popular fiction during the late 1800s.

dude—A western term used to describe a city-bred visitor.

flank attack—An attack on the left or right side of an enemy's formation.

frontier—A region just being opened to settlers.

goatee—A small, pointed beard that covers only the chin.

greenbacks—A slang term for United States paper money.

lasso—A long rope with a running noose at one end. Cowboys use lassos to catch horses and cattle.

mochila—The leather sheet used by Pony Express riders as a saddle cover and mail pouch.

Pony Express—An overland mail service that relied on relays of riders and horses to carry the mail.

quarantine—Enforced isolation of animals or people suspected of carrying a contagious disease.

roan—A bay, chestnut, or sorrel horse whose coat is sprinkled with white or gray.

rodeo—An exhibition of cowboy skills. Rodeo events include both riding and roping events.

saddletree—The wooden frame that gives a saddle its shape and stability.

scout—A skilled tracker and guide. Scouts ride ahead of a larger force to gather information about the terrain and the dangers that lie ahead.

seclusion—Staying hidden from public view.

sharpshooter—A marksman who demonstrates a high level of skill with a pistol or rifle.

sombrero—A Spanish name for a wide-brimmed hat that was popular in the Old West.

MORE GOOD READING ABOUT
BUFFALO BILL CODY

Burke, John. *Buffalo Bill: The Noblest Whiteskin*. New York: Putnam, 1973.

Cody, William F. *The Life of Hon. William F. Cody, Known as Buffalo Bill.* New York: Indian Head Books, 1991. Original edition 1879.

Garst, Shannon. *Buffalo Bill*. New York: Messner, 1948.

Robison, Nancy. *Buffalo Bill*. New York: Watts, 1991.

Russell, Don. *The Lives and Legends of Buffalo Bill*. Norman, Okla.: University of Oklahoma Press, 1960.

Sell, Henry Blackman, and Victor Weybright. *Buffalo Bill and the Wild West*. New York: Oxford University Press, 1955.

Smith, Robert Benjamin. "Face-Saving Skirmish at Warbonnet Creek," *Wild West* (October 1994), pp. 50–57.

Wheeler, Keith. "Idols in the Public Eye," in *The Scouts*. Alexandria, Va.: Time-Life Books, 1978, pp. 194–233.

Yost, Nellie Snyder. *Buffalo Bill: His Family, Friends, Fame, Failures, and Fortunes*. Chicago: Sage Books, 1979.

INDEX

A
Alexis, Grand Duke, 21–24

B
Baker, Johnny, 32
Billings, Horace (uncle), 11
Buntline, Ned, 19, 25–27

C
Campo Bonito mine, 39
Carson, Kit, 14
Carver, Dr. W. F., 30–31
Cedar Mountain, Wyoming, 40
Chrisman, George, 7
Civil War, 13–15
Cleveland, President Grover, 37
Cody, Arta (daughter), 26
Cody, Isaac (father), 9, 11–12
Cody, Julia (sister), 9
Cody, Kit Carson (son), 14, 26, 27
Cody, Louisa (wife), 15–16, 17, 25–26, 38, 40
Cody, Mary Ann (mother), 9, 12, 13, 14
Cody, Orra Maude (daughter), 26
Cody, Samuel (brother), 9
Cody, William (Buffalo Bill)
    acting career, 25–27, 29
    attitudes and
        personality, 9, 12, 14, 16, 20, 25, 28–29, 38, 40
    birth and childhood, 9–11
    buffalo hunter, 17–19
    conflicts with
        proslavers, 11–12
    Congressional Medal of Honor, 20
    death, 40
    description, 15, 32
    dime novels, 19
    education, 11–12
    farewell tour, 39
    and Grand Duke Alexis, 21–24
    homes and ranches, 27, 29, 39
    hotel owner, 16
    Kansas raiders, 13
    legacy, 41
    marries Louisa Federici, 15–16
    movie, 39–40
    and Native Americans, 19–20, 28–29
    nickname, 18–19
    overseas tours, 34–37, 38–39
    political career, 20
    Pony Express rider, 5–8
    as scout for Fifth

Cavalry, 19–20, 28–29
Seventh Kansas Volunteers, 14–15
travels with Sells-Floto Circus, 40
Wild West shows, 29, 30–33, 38–39
Cody, Wyoming, 39, 40
Comstock, Billy, 19
Custer, General George, 28

D
Denver, Colorado, 40

E
Earl's Court, Engand, 35
Edward, Prince of Wales, 35, 36

F
Fort Kearny, Nebraska, 12, 16
Fort Leavenworth, Kansas, 9, 11, 16

H
Hickok, Wild Bill, 14, 15, 27
Hyatt, Mary, 12

O
Oakley, Annie, 32–33, 34, 35
Omaha, Nebraska, 30

P
Pony Express, 5–8, 13, 32

S
Salsbury, Nate, 31
Sheridan, General Philip, 19, 21, 23
Sitting Bull, 28, 33
Slade, Alf, 7

Spotted Tail, 22, 23

T
Three Crossings, Wyoming, 7
Twain, Mark (Samuel Clemens), 32

W
War Bonnet Creek, 28
Willis, John, 12

V
Victoria, Queen, 35–36, 38

Y
Yellow Hair, 28–29